*further praise for* Feel Free

"Nick Laird's dazzling poems arrive with a kind of revolution-
ary candor; a truth-telling that's political, existential, and above
all, emotional. There is an implicit question mark after the title.
What is a good son, a good life? How does one navigate white-
ness, masculinity, grief? How does one feel free in his particular
body? This marvelous book is full of musical searching. *Feel Free*
is essential poetry."                                   —Terrance Hayes

"To call these poems immaculate, which they are, might swipe
away their hold on the human, the flawed, the fabricated, the
wobbles and outright wrongs running through the twenty-first
century as we've rendered it. But reading *Feel Free*, I feel myself
in the presence of a true master, a poet courageous and capable
enough to sing loss and shame, humor and praise as if it is all
part of the very same song. Which of course it is."
                                                        —Tracy K. Smith

"Nick Laird's acute eye and shades of meaning make these poems
a gift to read."                                        —*Guardian*

"The highlights of the book are love poems and city poems for
the Information Age: the poet's situations and relationships—as
a father, a son, a husband—are sized up and filtered through
different kinds of brilliantly manipulated language. . . . *Feel Free*
[is] Laird's best book yet."                            —*Irish Times*

"*Feel Free* reminds us of what poetry at its finest can be: challenging, politically engaged, humane, lyrical, infused with love of family and philosophical questions about self and soul."

—*Daily Mail*

"Is it possible to feel free when hemmed in by mortality? Laird's poetry offers a tentative 'yes' by way of skillful fluidity in the face of captivity." —*London Magazine*

"Formally, [Laird's] poems are neat and, at first glance, simple. But then they unfold, they unravel, and they are beautiful."

—*Manchester Review*

FEEL FREE

# NICK LAIRD

# Feel Free

Poems

W. W. NORTON & COMPANY
*Independent Publishers Since 1923*
NEW YORK / LONDON

Copyright © 2018 by Nick Laird
First American Edition 2019

First published in the UK by Faber & Faber Ltd

For information about permission to reproduce selections from this
book, write to Permissions, W. W. Norton & Company, Inc.,
500 Fifth Avenue, New York, NY 10110

For information about special discounts for bulk purchases, please
contact W. W. Norton Special Sales at specialsales@wwnorton.com
or 800-233-4830

Manufacturing by Sheridan

Library of Congress Cataloging-in-Publication Data

Names: Laird, Nick, 1975– author.
Title: Feel free : poems / Nick Laird.
Description: First American edition. | New York : W. W. Norton &
    Company, 2019.
Identifiers: LCCN 2019003522 | ISBN 9781324002741 (paperback)
Classification: LCC PR6112.A35 A6 2019 | DDC 821/.92—dc23
LC record available at https://lccn.loc.gov/2019003522

W. W. Norton & Company, Inc.
500 Fifth Avenue, New York, N.Y. 10110
www.wwnorton.com

W. W. Norton & Company Ltd.
15 Carlisle Street, London W1D 3BS

1 2 3 4 5 6 7 8 9 0

*In memory of CML*
*(1950–2017)*

# Acknowledgements

Many thanks to the editors of *Poetry, New Yorker, New York Times, Paris Review, Guardian, New York Review of Books, Poetry Review, Well Review, Poetry Ireland, Poetry London*, Bristol Festival of Ideas, Poem-a-Day, *Looking at the Stars* anthology, *Reading the Future: New Writing from Ireland*.

Many thanks to Alan Gillis, Vona Groarke, Zadie Smith, Don Paterson and Matthew Hollis.

Love and thanks to Z, and our children, Katherine and Harvey.

# Contents

iii

# FEEL FREE

i

# Glitch

More than ample, a deadfall of one metre eighty
to split my temple apart on the herringbone parquet,
and crash the OS, tripping an automated shutdown

in this specific case and halting all external workings
of the heated, moist robot I currently inhabit.
I am out cold for some time, and when my eyes roll in

you're there to help me over to our bed, as I explain
at length how taken I am with the place I'd been,
had been compelled to leave, airlifted out mid-gesture,

mid-sentence, risen of a sudden like a bubble
to the surface, a victim snatched and bundled out,
helplessly, from sunlight, the usual day, and all

particulars of my other life fled except the sense
that lasts for hours of being wanted somewhere else.

# To the Woman at the United Airlines Check-in Desk at Newark

Shonique, I am in time, and I know your fight
is hard: the fight is hard for everyone alive
and all those bodies in Departures

are naked under clothes and scarred –
that granted, even deeper scratches welt
and heal in days though still they smart

on contact, and I never really cared
for the terms I struck with earth,
more total war than limited skirmish.

I seethe, Shonique; I drink; I smoke weed
and seek relief from mental anguish;
the peopled life, car horns sounding down

on Houston. All three kinds of knowledge
fox me: outer, inner, pure mathematics –
but I understand your relatives are dying also

and I know the days are slow, the years fast,
that these are facts, however surprising.
Like you, I think the worst is yet to come;

plus, there's time lifting everything in sight,
Shonique, pocketing orchids and mothers,
the little white pebbledashed bungalows –

you in your small corner and me in mine.
Let me be clear and accommodative, more like
water than ice; and raise my hands to show

I mean no harm, and that I'm stupid,
and malicious, and if I'm trying to be fearless
I know it gives me no right to act like this.

What's understood is I'll be filed beneath
The Pricks, and fair enough. Very seldom
do I note the world wears a single face

with endless variations, and even then,
Shonique, it tends to be a face like yours,
one particularly fine. Speaking of which,

your fluorescent orange lipsticked lip
curls up at me with such distaste I have to sit
down now on my case at the rush of shame I feel:

and also love; and of course lust, hate, remorse.

# Fathers

We set a saucerful of water on the kitchen sill
and check it before breakfast for three days straight
until it's all evaporated. I think it's more like that.

*But don't you understand that Jesus lives in the sky?*
I think the moon is blown out, and the trees plucked
off the birthday cake and put back with the batteries,

and all the country of you divided up into the tiniest
of slices. But what I've got is microwave popcorn
and this ability to whistle every number one single

from 1987 onwards. There's no use getting all het
up: I give you a bed for your tiredness: I give you
some bread I have toasted and buttered: I give you

a stretch of the earth, baked hard, where we follow
the shiny beetle hauling the shield of himself into noon.
I can tuck a cloud under your chin. If it's an advert

the product is love. If it's an element, water. If it's
not consistent, that's part of its charm. If it's a bomb,
it's a beautiful dud, and I love you, she says, this much.

# The Good Son

*in my heart there was a kind of fighting*
*That would not let me sleep*

i

Remember me! demands the father's ghost,
and the deconstructionists gloss
that last request as 'Bring back my phallus' –
re-*member* me, as it were – and even after
Hamlet Sr stage-whispers his *Adieu!*
he hesitates, and asks his son again –
*Remember me* – since he can't help himself –
and Hamlet swears it on heaven and earth,
and is, by convention, meant there and then
to whip out his sword and avenge – but instead
he sits at the desk and unfastens his satchel
and takes out a pad and a quill to begin
getting it down in all its squalid detail,
which the Elizabethans deem a scandal.

But we did. We paid upfront and understood
that all accounts would soon be met
and every tab discharged in full.
Every loss incurred a debt
and hard to get the registers to balance.
This side of Cookstown Gospel Hall attests
in foot-long gothic font –
*For the Wages of Sin is Death . . .*
and a few yards round the corner,
nailed up in Monrush to a telegraph pole,
unfaded in its crude red,
white and blue lettering on plywood –
*Murder in Texas gets the electric chair.*
*In Magherafelt you get chair of the council.*

The rigour functioning in Sophocles as justice
we cannot retrofit with peace:
our animal language inadequate
to state in this state the state of the state.
Hard to think some companies
were simply unafraid
to leave aside
the long soliloquies:
*natural, simple, affecting*
Garrick had the whole fifth act rewritten
so when Claudius orders Hamlet
to set sail for England, his reaction
is to draw his blade, and let him have it.
I mean that Hamlet stabs him.

# Feel Free

To deal with all the sensational loss I like to interface
with Earth. I like to do this in a number of ways.
I like to feel the work I am exerting being changed,

the weight of my person refigured, and I like to hang
above the ground, thus; snorkelling, hammocks, alcohol.
I also like the mind to feel a kind of neutral buoyancy

and to that end I set aside a day a week, Shabbat,
to not act. Having ceded independence to the sunset
I will not be shaving, illuminating rooms or raising

the temperature of food. If occasionally I like to feel
the leavening of being near a much larger unnatural
tension, I walk off a Sunday through the high fields

of blanket bog, saxifrage, a few thin belted Galloways,
rounding Lough Mallon to stand by the form of beauty
upheld in a scrubby acre at Creggandevsky, where I do

duck and enter under a capstone mapped by rival empires
of yellow feather-moss and powdery white lichen: I like
then to stop, crouched, and press my back on a housing

of actual rock, coldness which lives for a while on the skin.
And I like when I give you the nightfeed, Harvey, how you're
concentrating on it: fists clenched, eyes shut, like this *is* bliss.

I like a steady disruption. I like it when the solid mantle turns
to shingle and water rushes up it over and over, in love.
My white-noise machine from Argos is set to Crashing Wave

but I'm not averse to the presence of numerous and minute
quanta moving very fast in unison; occasions when a light
wind undulates the ears of wheat, or a hessian sack of pearl

barley seed is sliced with a pocket knife and pours. I like
the way it sounds pattering on stone. I like how the starlings
over Monti cohere and separate their bodies into one
   cyclonic

symphony, and I like that the hawk of the mind catches at
their purse, pulse, caul, arc. I like the excitation passing as
a shadow-ripple back and how the bag is snatched, rolls

slack; straight; falciform; mouthing; bulbing; a pumping
heart. I like to interface with millions of coloured pixels
depicting attractive people procreating on a screen itself

dependent on rare metals mined by mud-grey children
who trudge up bamboo scaffolding above a greyish-red lake
of belching mud. I like how the furnace burning earth instils

in me reflexive gestures of timidity, self-pity and deference
as I walk across the kinder surfaces, grass, say, or sand,
unable ever to meet with my eyes the gaze of the sun.

iii

I can imagine that my first and fifth marriages will be
to the same human, a woman, the first marriage working
well enough that we decide to try again as soon as it's,

you know, mutually convenient. I can see that. I like the fact
we're 'supercooled starmatter', even if I can't envisage you
as anything other than warm and bleating. The thing is

I can be persuaded fairly easily to initiate immune responses
by the fake safety signals of national anthems, cleavage,
     family
photographs, country lanes, large-eyed mammals, fireworks,

the King James Bible, Nina Simone singing 'The Twelfth of
     Never',
cave paintings, coffins, dolphins, dolmens. But I like it also
when the fat impasto of the canvas gets slashed by a tourist

with a claw hammer, and a glimpse is caught of what you
     couldn't
say. Entanglement I like, spooky action at a distance
     analogising
some little thing including this long glance across the
     escalators

or how you know the song before you switch the station on.
When a photon of light meets a half-silvered mirror and
     splits
one meets the superposition of two, being twinned: and this
     repeats.

Tickling your back, Katherine, to get you to sleep, I like to
    lie here
with my eyes closed and think about my schoolfriends'
    houses before
choosing one to walk through slowly, room by sunlit room.

# Grenfell

*i.m.*

Please rate your experience of your experience.
Overall, would you say you're pleased; mostly
pleased; neutral; displeased; or not pleased at all?
Would you recommend our business to a friend?

Would you say this evening light falls against
the tower in a manner conducive to your happiness
or not that at all? Would you say all members
of the union are rotten with despair? Priced in

hours, how far from there do you think we are?
If you can, please provide a detailed description
of the structure you were born in, the early drafts,
the texture, the facilities of selves who go about

their day in you, and if indicating age and race
and gender, a sexual preference, a religion,
educational attainment and household income,
I think we know each other well enough by now

to take it that we understand those purely as
contingent states, one's desires being mappable
on strangers, always. All the bodies are bodies
of water, regardless of terms and conditions,

of energy ordered to what is the matter.
Please rate your last real day on a scale of one
to ten where one is utter dullsville and ten
adjusts the contrast setting permanently upwards.

How satisfied are you with customer support?
Please evaluate the final minutes for how one
might account for it. Any additional comments
should be left in the space at the foot of this page

and all of the following pages.

# Parenthesis

I lie here like the closing bracket on the ledger of the
　　mattress.
Asleep between us the children are hyphens – one hyphen,
　　one underscore –
and it takes a few moments at five a.m. to get it quite
　　straight that
what I thought was my name being called is the dog at my
　　feet snoring.

Asleep between us, the children, our hyphens (one hyphen,
　　one underscore),
know love is a paragraph lacking an ending and typeset by
　　hand in italics.
What I thought was my name being called is the dog at my
　　feet snoring
and it's alright to collapse like that, like a marquee gone
　　into its final sigh.

No love is a paragraph lacking an ending and typeset by
　　hand in italics.
It is an ellipsis of three drops of Night Nurse that leaves
　　the pillow sticky
and it's alright to collapse like that, like a marquee gone
　　into its final sigh,
like my mother in the hard return of a long death and the
　　stanza break.

It is an ellipsis of three drops of Night Nurse that leaves
 the pillow sticky.
I lie here like the closing bracket on the ledger of the
 mattress,
like my mother in the hard return of a long death and the
 stanza break,
and it takes a few moments at five a.m. to get it quite
 straight, that.

# Silk Cut

I was five and stood beside my dad
at a junction somewhere in Dublin
when I slipped my hand in his
and met the red end of a cigarette

but now our hearts are broken
we walk down to the Braeside
where we can get a proper pint
and his voice tears up a bit

about the emptiness in the house
and we are going home, waiting
at the turn for the traffic, when I find
I have to stop my hand from taking his

# Manners

I am interested in the possibility of reasonable conduct.
Reasonable conduct is part of the ordinary course of things.
Also violence, though one must resist this. Death is only life

at one remove, hanging from a metal hook, wrapped around
with tissue paper and a forty long and waves of sound
and waves of light and graduating waves. The small engines

meant for this, meant to slide electrons of the universe
about their electronic grid, are us. If I try to see it, I see it
as a version of one of those gridded puzzles with a piece

missing, where you move a piece up and across and down,
and so on, to try to make a picture, but in this case
there is no picture to aim for, and the puzzle is at least 3D.

The puzzle itself is the picture, you are the gap, an instance
of peckishness or nausea or flames or lilies or bathwater.
Also quickened with touches of transporting grief and love.

I hold mine out now in front as a black single-breasted suit
I inspect to check that it is suitable for wearing to the funeral.
I am slapping dust from its shoulders. If we're so suspicious

of meaning, Dragos, that's because meaning has, historically,
had very hard edges. The point remains however: it is to be
the other, not to reiterate how I am not you, and never can be.

I know that already. But I get up in the morning and break
fast. I am still burning toast. I am taken with the possibilities
of radical formal shifts and tonal ambiguities. And I require

ceremony to practice ending properly. I know if you made me
dwell on it long enough I could feel bad about the death
of that clothes moth that just fluttered out from the suitbag.

# Autocomplete

I expect the holy of holies must be
to watch machinery making machinery,

no? Begin with the others and do what they do,
and later you can branch off into the fresh

snow. Did you think the room smelt of not
having been smoked in? Or that her face

was the gate of a pool after closing? The wax seal
began as a personal stamp of authenticity

before it grew into a tool the administrators
used to represent you. Freehold of the soul

meant setting up the product line across all
the different platforms, and what I would like

to do is swim in you, it's true, and I would add
that you are free to look me in the eyes when I do

so

# The Vehicle and the Tenor

When it comes at me in the mirror with its meaning
ramping up until it passes and lowers in pitch, I'm on
the bit of the M1 where it bisects the Ring of Gullion

and I switch lanes, and let my right foot alleviate
its weight on the accelerator of the Focus,
and the ambulance is faster, and the shift in its report

an effect of the change in the wave's frequency
and length on the observer, who is, in this case, me,
heading up to Newry hospice off the red-eye, and I

lag and have to have the window down for brisk air.
If the grief moves in towards me at high speed,
the wavelengths I observe are decreased as the frequency

increases. I don't know what this means though
I can tell you how it feels: in the cryptic centre
of my head a voice recites a rhyme I read somewhere

or heard once or otherwise made up:
*Let us go to the woods*, one little pig cries.
*But why would we do that?* his brother replies.

*To look for my mother*, the little pig cries.
*But why would we do that?* his sister replies.
*For to kiss her to death*, the little pig whispers.

What is driving along this but a guided dream
since the road feeds itself in as the planed length
time feeds to the mind's lathe to get it trimmed

correctly to size: heavy clouds; the waterlogged
fields; a rainbow arcing faintly out to the west
and I keep that with everything I keep to myself.

I am either in the midst of it or on my own or both
things are true at the same time. I kill the radio.
Were the universe to finish, music would endure

though I have no memories left for the moment before
so when I think of you I think of you sat slumping
on the edge of the mattress, zonked on Zopiclone,

small and bald as a wee scaldy fallen out the nest
and found there hours after you were meant
to have gone on to bed. At my coming in

you barely raise your head, your eyes are half-shut
and you cannot find the holes for the buttons
on your nightie, because you have it on you inside out.

I know every journey to a source is homecoming,
and I am bombing along the District of Songs,
along the Great Road of the Fews, towards you,

through a depression left by the caldera's collapse.
This is the District of Poets, the district of the Dorsey:
*Doirse* meaning doors or gates, the solitary pass

to the old kingdom through the earthworks' long
involvement, a pair of abrupt Iron Age banks
running parallel for a mile or so. An entrenchment.

An entrance. All manner and slant of analogy etcetera
but when, in the end, we had kissed you to death,
we sat and held your cold hands for a half hour more

and wiped with tissues all the black stuff bubbling up
from your lungs away from your lips, and wept
a good bit, and got up then and folded your clothes

and stacked your cards and binned the flowers,
and I sat out there in my rental car in the car park
as you kept on lying in here, past all metaphor,

left by yourself on the cleared stage like a real corpse.

ii

# Parable of the Arrow

Imagine it is dusk and there are two men – friends, but not
particularly close – walking through the bamboo grove,
leading a litter of pigs back to the camp. Out of nowhere
the older man is struck in the chest by an arrow and falls.

The friend tells him he must pull the arrow out and clean
the wound.

The man replies he cannot let the arrow be removed
until he gets to know it better, until he grasps its proper
nature as a clawed or razor arrow. He must establish if the
shaft is a karavira sapling or flighted with the feather of
a heron, or a peacock, if it's fastened with the tendon of a
ruru deer or a temple monkey –

The friend explains that at this time these are not his main
concerns.

The man insists he has a right to know his assailant's age
and height, the colour of his eyes, what debt or threat
or great disaster should bring him to this pass, whether
his aggressor hails from such and such a caste, and if he
intends to sleep well or rise late and feel guilt or free.

The friend says keep still.

The man is adamant. He wants to know if the one who tried to kill him is all kindness with his children, and his children's children, and their friends and so on, and how far does his circle run, and does he recognise by now it should have looped the earth?

The friend says bite down on this here belt.

# The Good Son

*Passive suffering is not a theme for poetry . . .*

i

Your own neighbour at it to get you out.
I was stood in the bath with a bill-hook
as the glass shattered and they screamed threats,
that same auld slander and terrible muck.
The childer was all small then. Even the police,
they told us to leave. I mind we lay on the ground.
He was with them, laughing, done up like a priest,
and my daddy got his shotgun and opened
the bedroom window and clipped one of them.
We knew it was him alright by the limp.
All those years we lived in Newtownhamilton
and Whitecross sure I never lay down.
I would've come home from work and slept in
the chair but at first dark got up again.

## ii

The time they got my sister's man
she identified the boy: many's the time he'd been
in her kitchen and had his dinner. He ran
bandsaws with her husband in the timber yard
and they shot Roy in the head and fired off
shots across him and him already dead.
He'd a great dog. D'you mind the dog he had?
Brung up from a pup he found in a hedge.
Pepper. Pepper was got out in the graveyard
trying to dig Roy up the night he was laid.
He shot at the dog too but missed and was lifted.
Ten years and he did one. In the courthouse
he said nothing till she looked him right in the face.
*Alison, they made me do it. I was made.*

The time they were after Joe McCullough
he fought them in and out of his bungalow.
Blood everywhere. He would have been alright
only one of them went over and slit his throat.
Then they put a booby-trap bomb on him
and a sow pig knocked it and got blew to bits.
And Thomas McConnell. They were hid
on the roof of his tin shed waiting on him.
You know a fella came to our Hall about a year ago
wanting the youngest to go and do silage.
Gareth took the boy aside and said,
*D'you know who that is?* It was some goon
working for Dessie O'Hare's crowd, and like a cod,
only for that, he would've gone.

# Coppa Italia

If I prefer to drink in Irish pubs in non-Irish nations
it's because misquotations are more revealing
and Tino and Patrick are stood at the bar.

It is Saturday and late in the desert of the real.
The table I like best is out on the cobbles,
a plastic red table with a plastic tablecloth

attached to it with metal clips. The laminate
is stamped with the *trompe l'œil* of the gaps
and fretwork of a real cast-iron table. Inside,

waiting for the pints to settle, a violence on
the small bright pitch. A man in blue and a man
in a red shirt float, collide, collapse and rise

as one thing turned on itself; are held apart
and shouted down and striding back beneath
the floods blue is distraught, a sacker of cities,

but when the camera pans to red he's laughing,
supple and sleek and lit like a stamen at the very
centre of a long four-petalled shadow, waiting

for the ball to pollinate him, deep in their half.

# User

The only Novacell was in the kitchen so I hesitated
before ambling down the hall and glancing in our Bean
to check that Yip was Uberliving©, ironing Ken's blouses

and co-hosting a Meet-and-Greet for Bebop enthusiasts,
a form of Original Music she'd quite recently Addicted to.
I slipped in and flicked the MoodChute, whispered the visor's

name onto the Eardrive and hollowed at his off-site.
Overall, demazing: semi-helpful; size, age, tribal appearance
not dissimilar to mine though he was just 28 percent

Blasian and had won Freestyle Bronze in 4-6-Summer
on the PetSafe moon of the Eternal Insurance System®.
I de-acked the stream and saw his temples were greying,

indicating wilting, and that he could do with a TreatWeek
in a JumpCoat© to vigorate the T's. Underwhelmed when
memflicking to find it 10-80 since he'd stoked. As he coded

The Sunrise Raisinana Patch™, allowing a fourteen mil
boost in the laterals to stave off the worst, I impressioned
taking a QuantiCation© with his extended, and why not try

the Salted Leaps on the Rio Seven islets, since I always liked
to jellifish. It was sufficient to just float there and feel
nothing, no language for it, just be unformatted, and free.

# On Not Having Children

*for AJ*

The most difficult operation to stage is the retreat.

There's a book of the Bible where God is not mentioned.

The water in your tumbler is older than the sun.

If the word 'attention' was not Chaucer's invention

his use of it is the earliest we have extant in manuscript

and there are words that lack rhymes: silver; month;

depth; false. It makes them immune to doggerel

but also to the ballad form.

# Watermelon Seed

If you extract the compact planet,
roughly sketched with jungle, wetlands,
I pick a knife with which to split it
and you put back the jams and ketchup.
The substantial rind is very chilly,
the flesh wet cotton candy cleanly
parted on the pressured edge to paired
slabs of seeded red, undersown by more
seeds that face eviction by your fork.
I like watching you at work: one dangles
from a tine, expelled and slickly black,
suspended by a tendril of thin pink pulp till
you flick it with your index finger
expertly at the sink. Plink.

# La Méditerranée

In the midst of our lifelike life
I come to this fork in your hand –
stainless silver, of appreciable weight –

and I fully understand its pronginess,
the bent of want, an expressive head
and narrow neck spreading

like a delta out to three strict parallels.
You, the children, me.
At some point the waiter brought

your sea bass and the fork hovers over
its seared arrangement of chainmail,
its lips parted in surprise.

Against the stiff table linen
and sunlight on the knife
your skin is caramel and scuffed

a little whitely at the knuckles.
A few veins give the skin
its dark ridges and where each hair

plants itself there is a small dent
and crinkle in the flesh.
If the situation is not stable

nor sustainable,
what I want to mention is
if we did continue further in –

into an atom of the flesh
or the metallic fabric of the fork,
the micro-weft of the tablecloth,

it would be more or less the same
kind of utter emptiness –
as at the heart of any restaurant

there is this dead eye
of the sea bass on your plate,
its aureole lens, its lightless pupil

sunk flush as a thumb tack holding
the universe itself in place
and I stare at it, and it stares back.

# Chronos

I swim to earn endorphins and eat my greens
because I need the fibre and the vitamins.

I shoot and kill eleven wolves
to barter with the skins.

I do my best to clean the bath,
then separate the bodies of the zombies

from their faces with a crowbar
or a chainsaw,

and make it to the water tower –
but out of the flames of the jack-knifed lorry

lurches the Overlord Zombie –
who will not ever stop –

and already is upon me
gorging himself on my delicate neck.

# XY

When I slide it in the slot to press
the buttons in their order, wait,
I'm empire-building. Damn straight.
I'm Genghis Khan. Yes ma'am. I guess
I am embarrassing. I guess I'm done.
Maybe nothing beats the nothingness.
Maybe all I need is this depletion
and not French poems or drunk chess.
Maybe I take the antihistamine
and it doesn't stop me operating.
Simple physics, Little Richard.
If my appetite intensifies my vigilance
I'd say that's my lookout, and my business.
Then I'd say, here, take my card.

# The Cartoons

When my head was on fire I googled fire
and the first result described it as
a rapid oxidation releasing heat and light
and various reaction products
like sleeplessness and these poems.

I had had enough of going in and out
of doorways. Being undecided
was only like existing on two or more
floors at the same time. Which is like
reading. Or parenting. Or being alive,

on the outside and the flipside, here
where you are listening to me talk
and to your continuous response,
continuous as a river is, as my
father when he drives, reifying

things by saying them out loud.
Some cows. The cheese factory.
Declan Cosgrove's house.
*You know who else is in some pain?*
*Everyone, and all the time.*

I need to sit here very still in this
room where I am allowed to be this
still for a few minutes with the traffic
lit by the periodic lift and tilt of sirens
or my daughter coughing next door

and then I need to sit on the sofa,
and let the youngest take my face
in his hot hands again and pull me in
until we're nose to nose and say over
and over, 'Daddy, listen to me.'

# Team Me

I get very bored of having to respond
to the circumstances of my own life.
I'm tired of trailing my ego around.

I remember the feeling from being a lawyer,
sat there in front of some client thinking
I just can't represent this cunt much longer.

Most nights we meet each other face to face –
at civil dusk, in defeat, my little regent
standing in Gristedes's dairy aisle or the lower

field where the red clay banks and falls away,
and the stream that feeds the Ballinderry slows
on shallow gravels. Wherever. On his own.

Always with the narrow back set like a shield
against me, his shadow like a bracket or a lever
twice as long as him, and half as thin,

keeping him forever perpendicular to earth.
He turns. Bat-fangs. Bowl cut. Such pretty little
ears that hold the crown, a ripped green cracker hat

from Christmas 1983. O my petty liege.
My bliss and dearest enmity. My nemesis.
When he spots me now and slopes across,

affecting a limp, because he's depressed,
what I say when he asks how it went on the whole
is *no really no really no you were amazing*

# Incantation

Because we time-travel into the future
at a blistering sixty minutes an hour,
I ask you to sit down and write me
one beautiful sentence I might carry
in my pocket on the journey when I go,
and in the window of the train unfold

*O you were the best of all my days.*

Never knowing if the thing is broken
or the door between us is still open,
you would like me to sit down and write
you one beautiful sentence you might
carry in your wallet when you leave,
and in the cab you take it out and read

*Permit me voyage, love, into your hands.*

Depending where one stands, each circle
back is a possible fall, a fail, a spiral,
and I would like you to take a few seconds
to write me out one beautiful sentence
to carry now across the night and ocean,
and held up at the gate I sit down and open

*Everything was beautiful and nothing hurt.*

iii

# Cinna the Poet

I was trying to write like an adult.
I had children.
I was at the end of something.

As I waited at my table by the window for the coffee,
I saw that the Sirocco had deposited
a scrim of dust on the sill overnight,
and it was the dark red of powdered blood,
and like any of the others of my kind would have done,
I graffitied it.

In the past I might have gone for a peace sign
or a smiley face or an ejaculating penis,
but today I scrawled my name in it
and my vocation,
and left my fingertip ferrous with desert.

It felt like stroking suede against the nap,
half illicit, the particulates milled by wind
and sieved by the distance
to the softness of ash or brick-dust.

I had been adding and subtracting
sounds from my epic on the winds
that thread the known world,
but something like a real poem surfaced
then, in the dust,
in my letters edged with tiny drifts.

What I wanted in a small thing was some
principle, some vividness
that lived both in things small and things great.

A desert is red and the dust is red
because the stones that make it up were red.
It is the iron staged within.
They share the rationale of blood.

The tone was off.
They understand the colour of

Lucinda was filling my demi-tasse
and stopped to watch the man,
a partisan, standing in the square outside the window.
The red cap of all his tribe was too small for his head
which wobbled like a tied balloon
as he read the name I'd written on the sill.

At the nearer counter Kestius, mad again,
stopped reciting his ode to prostitutes
and turned around to get a proper look.

I had been thinking how the coffee
pouring from the spout and stopping
was not unlike
the
thick
tail
of
a
black
rat
flickering into a drain,
and I wasn't listening, and he said it again.

My Death is standing outside the window
carrying on his shoulder a leg of lamb
rolled in darkened butcher paper
and My Death is upset
and pointing his cigarette at me.

How they massed in the streets for their Caesar,
that rapist, that racist, that fat
narcissist
who found the crowd responded best to flattery
and three-word phrases
framed as an imperative.

I do not believe in the imagined realm of perfectness,
where nothing ever changes, where everything simply is,
and which, according to Plato and Judeo Christian
    philosophy,
is the true realm of nature; the sense experience,
the red dust, the coffee, the leg of lamb – merely
    illusory.

We have no reason to believe in the perfect circle.
We have no reason to believe justice exists.
There is the endless play of absence and presence.
Seasons. Tides. The moon.

I stood up and knocked my notebooks off the table.

Long ago I noted the impossibility of imagining
a heaven that doesn't bore us instantly
to death, and I don't believe the human body
is really a luminous body of white light
that moves towards the larger light
when it dies.

On the odd occasion I feel amazed to be alive
though not often, to be honest, and not recently.

Last summer when the weather optioned its menace
his priests summoned those born feet first,
the albinos, the twins,
those afflicted with harelips.

I lived in a state of despair and rage, we all did.
I could not remember the last time the political
had come to bear on the personal
to such a large extent, and I grew up
in the civil war,
sitting reading how the world's tallest man
had saved a dolphin
or they'd designed a gun for women –
to be shot by women, not to shoot them.

Last week, after the purge,
Kestius stopped me in the toilets to tell me
how he'd sealed his major poems in earthen jars
and buried them at nightfall by the lilac in his garden.

The time is just too real, he said.
We are approaching the source, he said.
Don't you detect its heat in the night air,
in the vividness beneath the skin,
how everything is frantic.

        Now their leader was dead
and his supporters on fire and I stood,
at a loss, on the edge of their anger –
you have been there – watching the dark
present dispose
itself too easily and flow away from me.

I could not pass
and when the girl ran up and spat
panic like a swarm of bees and I tried
to escape and slipped
on my papers and fell and hit my head
on the stone steps.

The flesh is not a vessel emptied out at death.
I had the evidence of my own parents.

Black stuff bubbles from the lungs to the lips.

Why would anyone set aside deities born of this earth,
that protect the place, to privilege metaphysical
divinities
who do not have that relationship?

Sirocco. Mistral. Levante. Ostro.

None of them functioned as names exactly,
not without following the sighing in the eaves
or a rounding in the branches.

But I was unsure what to do with those
sounds, and such information,
unsure what to do with the inconstancy of things in
    general.

        Poetry had not been good for me.

It hardened me where I should have been
otherwise.
What is it anyway to say that one thing
is like another? I practise forms of accusation.

[53]

I came to as they were dousing me in lamp oil.
Kestius was howling like a dog and being held back.
The girl was going through my bag.

I watched My Death try and strike a match.

# The Folding

i

In the midst of this lifelike grief
I am stood at the cutlery drawer,
and keep on standing here as if
I might remember what I came in for,
but then I think of something else,
and head upstairs only to forget
what that was and find myself

eyeing the unmade bed, the bookshelves,
the snow still coming down outside
and realise then, and lift a stack
of printer paper and the safety scissors
for the kids to make snowflakes
I'll tape to the kitchen windows,
since that was what my mother did.

ii

I know in terms of cuts and folds
a modest pattern's adequate,
that infinite complexity's composed
by simple rules, and the last was that
you had to live it out, right to the end –
even as your body starts to stop,
as your face withdraws from itself

and your eyes continue, trapped,
braving a last turn about the place.
O that dull, almost inaudible pat
of obliterative fleck on the glass,
and the clock, and the held breath
as the kids concentrate on symmetries
or the blades' irresistible path.

iii

I am four and follow her until I spot
        the photo booth and slip inside
to climb up on the spinny seat, and watch
        cartoons that do not start, and wait
            for forty years as they raze
    the aisles and checkouts, the car park,
    wait for her to draw back the dark

    and find me here, staring at the screen
where what I learn of absence is the panic
    is substantial, the face is lit with tears
        and snot and everyone is crying
            as I fold myself into her skirt,
        unable to explain that I was here,
        behind the curtain, the whole time.

iv

Civil dusk. I scrape the plates.
The falling's softened to a waltz
and the garden's lit lavender white.
I suit them up like astronauts
and we step out through the airlock
to a scene as soundproofed as a dream:
its padded walls and ceiling are being

shredded without end. A snowflake catches
in her mother's lashes when Katherine's
looking upwards through the branches
at the sky, at the unfolding of bright
wave on bright wave, coherent scrims
of fast scantlings looking to alight, alive,
and we hold out our hands until they are white.

# New York ElastiCity

When the hand is red,
some of the walkers pause
& others continue,
some of the vehicles pause
& others continue,
& I am no longer that
clerk to the heir of etc.
& something of this city's
brute capacity for gathering
is like a shining in my head.

The valleys of glass & reset
stone have softer, smaller
forces pushing through them
with shopping bags like pollen
sacs attached to their bodies.
Happiness is only a state
of utter absorption,
so why not take an island,
not large, & see the people
of the world live together there?

I notice first they put the brown
people in brown shirts
& made them stand behind
the counter in Starbucks as
the customers are played by whites
& east Asian girls. Each
consciousness enacts its own
drama in the silence of
a breathing mind till Ahmed,
the barista, calls your name.

On Mercer & Bleecker
the jackhammers answer
& a rising siren answers
but what I'd like to listen to is rain,
no? The plainness of its thinking,
the fat splatter of the first ripe drops
on the hot sidewalk, its hiss,
its consistence, its soft-shoe shuffle –
the grid clearing & darkening
as the Atlantic rolls in.

# Getting Out the White Vote

Because of the unfairness I resigned.
I mean I re-signed for another stint in
the inferno's furnace, with a furlough
on the Vegas strip. Hell, I deserved it.

I dreamt the real war waged in corridors
of server banks in hangars in New Jersey
or Missouri never happened, or happened
only in my dream. You hadn't heard me.

I couldn't help myself so I helped myself,
and when I told you to replace it,
I meant put it back to what it was.
I never said that you could change it.

# The Good Son

They disappeared. / They were disappeared.
Argentina pioneered the passive use of active verbs,
though the Stalinist regime
had a similar irregular inflection
when a member of the nomenklatura
'was stepped down'.

Physical force is nominalising.

You do not speak but you are spoken,
and the force, if exercised without curb,
is able to transmute the bodies into corpses.

We are aware there are two forces –

one that kills, and one that does not, not yet,
for now is merely fiddling with the implement
it might bring down this every instant.

She sighs; she lives; she has a soul and yet
she is a thing, a thing that has a soul. Mirror.

Extraordinary – and how does the soul inhabit
an extraordinary house, how much does it cost,
instant by instant, to accommodate
itself to such a place, this extraordinariness,
such writhing being requisite, so much bending
and folding and pleating and snipping and so on
required of it constantly. Door. Stairs.

She simplifies down to whatever you wish, even if
the soul was not made who could live inside a thing. Front
door. Shadowed glass. If it does so, under the pressure
of necessity, there is not one element of its nature
to which violence is not done.

# Temple of Last Resort

I wanted the real God to turn up and say

*I was just kidding.*

*About everything.*

*I was just kidding.*

*That guy's my idiot brother.*

*Ignore him. He's an asshole.*

# Crunch

It's clear that Schwarzenegger was the acceptable exploration
   of the Nazis
and the red embroidered velvet book is chained up to the
   lectern but
you insist that human skin contains so many receptors for
   gentle pressure,
deep pressure, sustained pressure, follicle bending and
   minute vibration
that all the edges will get rounded down eventually and no
   one ignorant
of history ever re-enter. I say if you miss the actual earth
   you should sink
your fingers in the soil of the rabbit foot fern I keep on my
   desk and water
almost never from my thermos of black tea. You say
   Nevada palominos
at a gallop hundreds strong draw the same subsiding trail
   of pinkish dust
across the monotheistic desert as when the Christians took
   back Spain
or Dylan went electric, and I say saying everything at once
   is not the same
as saying nothing. Lightning is a brief but necessary
   corrective to the system's
electrical imbalance, though you say the sirens are becoming
   more frequent
and the air outside itches your eyes and causes them to
   weep a gluey substance
in the night. I say it's an area of low pressure. You say it's
   a feature not a bug.

I say maybe some species can be successfully domesticated
and some just can't.
Deer, for instance, prove remarkably resistant. I turn the
sound down and listen.
This morning I was taken with an origin myth where the
giant vomits up the earth
only after great pain in his stomach. The golden plover
with its two-note song
is the prime glossator of our time – left, right, black, white
– though in real life
the Zermelo set neutrinos pass through does include you.
You are really very busy
with your multi-volume study of the strictly curtailed –
Dunwich, Minoa, Tunguska,
Chernobyl. I say the lizard also spat the sun back out
though no, I don't believe
the Hopi chose the desert so they'd never have to not pray
for rain. I agree it is
insane. I recommend the moment Pliny held a naked flame
against an amber bead
and smelt the tang of pine, and knew it to be resin not a
teardrop wept by Neptune.
You ask if the word (peoples) is grammatically correct?
I say all the signs conspire
to suggest that an inflection point is coming. You claim
nothing fucks you like time.
I say just because I'm shouting doesn't make me wrong.
You think we need to call
someone. I say I stayed with a warlord in Split who had
the given name of Dragon
and a perfectly serviceable coffee table constructed from
four upstanding shell
casings and a square pane of tempered glass. I say poetry
is weather for the mind

not an umbrella. I say take Star of Bethlehem for shock,
  mustard seed for the deep
gloom occasioned for no earthly reason. You'd like to see
  me alphabetised into
my rightful places and the files archived. I'd have you used
  in combinations of
the adjectives and verbs and nouns I'm certain you deserve.
  You say drought it was
that first gifted us the arch, aqueducts with strict declivities
  of inches to the mile
but I say Byzantium was nothing but expansionist slavers
  and ingenious trash
and the vaulted roof of Wells cathedral leaves me as
  impressively empty. You say
the thing with leaving is you have to go somewhere. I am
  well aware my semen is
an avalanche engulfing unsuspecting lunchers on the
  terrace, après-ski. I am sorry
when I cough I cough up all this black stuff. You say it is
  invisible from space.
I ask have you noticed in the grace of Duncan Edwards an
  anonymity of style
true to both his kind and his kind of generation? You say
  the children are listening.
We keep on glimpsing the doe and her fawn at the edge of
  the clearing at dawn,
and for thousands of years. I say it's not so much cricket
  that's a metaphor for life
but the other way round. I say my father says the one time
  he saw his own father cry
was after the Munich Air Disaster. You say of Pangu, when
  he died, that his voice
became the thunder and his flesh became the earth, his
  hair the trees, his sweat

the rain, his bones the rocks and monuments, and in the
    end the rest of us were left
as little glossy insects to graze upon his body. I say we
    need to keep each other close
and whisper. You say one must be heavy as an engine not
    a rock. I say the working
parts operate at such a pitch they're silent – and at this
    point in the argument you make
a kind of grunt.

# Horizontal Fall

Once in the suburbs outside Providence
an abundant week-old snow compounded
to a single sheet of large gardens and scant
woods and there –

three deer bounding suddenly alongside –

and once in extended eye contact when
Opposite shouldered off her jacket
and opened up on tiptoe the overhead locker –

and now on the elevated line through Harlem,
the cold shallows of its bright streets beneath
and the lights in the whole train shutting off
suddenly, all the lights shutting off suddenly,
serpentine brakes roused then ended in a creak
and silence –

and the assorted breathing bodies

about to start incorporating
coats and bags and phones – but something in us
wanting to remain sitting there at large
and almost unelaborated in the dark carriage

# Extra Life

Press esc and wait. White
light. Five tender reports.
You are in a new room
and Father has gone missing.
Mother suffers but does nothing,

watches television, weeps.
Your avatar is – it doesn't matter.
Basil, Fatou, Ahmed,
do you choose country A or B?
A is cheaper but more risky;

the living conditions are poor,
the onward journey by sea.
If you choose B you have a chance
of reaching C by land
but now the trafficker demands

the fee up front, in cash,
and you distrust the way he laughs.
Click here if you sleep for a week
in a concrete shaft and then go
back and ask. Click here to beg.

Get on a truck for a hundred hours.
The desert is a thousand miles.
The stars are numberless and very
close. Sleep in fits and starts. Sleep
sitting up. Take it in turns to sleep.

Click here if you get robbed.
Click here if you get raped.
Click here if you get caught.
Click here if you're sent back
or held for an indefinite term

in a 'processing facility'.
Press esc and wait. White
light. Your character appears.
Click here to hop the fence
and merge with the foot passengers.

As you dock, click to watch
the iron maw descend on scores
of border agents, waiting.
Click to turn the keys left
in the ignition, and ride the Harley

off the ramp and into Dover,
and park it by the cop shop,
and inside hand the keys across,
saying, 'This is not my motor bike.'
Click to shiver through the night

on a mattress of catalogues
and pallets by the bottle bins
in the carpark of the Argos
on Cricklewood Broadway.
Press esc and wait. White light.

Track the acrobatic Sub-Saharan
dodging through the gridlocked
traffic. Click <u>here</u> to crowbar
open the articulated truck
and board it. Press esc and wait.

White light. Watch the boat inflate.
<u>Click</u> twice to make it float.
<u>Click</u> to lift your kids in. <u>Click</u>
to lift your wife. The sea is level
as a puddle until backwash

from the tanker hits and panic
tips you in. Down you go and further
so the vice of water tightens
till your chest and spine will surely
snap. Click <u>here</u> to save.

<u>Click</u> to bring your children
back. <u>Click</u> to kiss them
on their lips. <u>Click</u> to resurrect
your wife and pick
the seaweed from her hair.

# To His Soul

Old ghost, my one guest,
heckler, cajoler, soft-soaper
drifting like smoke down
the windowless corridor,

the jailer is shaking his keys out,

and you will soon depart for
lodgings that lack colour
and where no one will know
how to take your jokes.


*After Hadrian*

# Notes

'Autocomplete' repurposes a couple of lines from the notebooks of Geoffrey Madan.

'Incantation' includes lines by Frank O'Hara, Hart Crane and Kurt Vonnegut.